THE POST OFFICE

Charles Olson

THE POST OFFICE

A Memoir of His Father

With an Introduction by George F. Butterick

Grey Fox Press
San Francisco

"Stocking Cap" was first published in the summer 1951 issue of *Montevallo Review*; in 1966 it was issued as Writing 13 by the Four Seasons Foundation.

Book design and composition by Zoe Brown.

Second Printing, 1984

Cover photograph: Charles Olson as infant in his father's mailbag; courtesy the Charles Olson Archives (through the kindness of Mrs. John Sullivan of Worcester, Mass.).

Library of Congress Catalog Card Number: 74-75456

ISBN 0-912516-14-3

Distributed by The Subterranean Company,
P. O. Box 10233, Eugene, Oregon 97440.

Manufactured in the United States of America

CONTENTS

INTRODUCTION

It was apparently to be a *book* on his father (he referred to it in conversation as a "book"), which he never completed. He writes in an entry dated March 8, 1948 in a notebook: "At least one course is clear—do this book on yr father without reference to culture—style, manner, tricks—do it on the level of mediocre humanitas. If you are not an artist, genius, & clever, let this make it clear. And take the consequences." (He had written earlier, as part of a deeply introspective passage, "For this whoring after culture on my part is a path by which I continue to be a son, & fail to take up my own perceptions & malehood.")

All three stories were written early in 1948, after Olson had returned to Washington following his research venture to the west coast for material towards a book on the American west he hoped to write and for which he obtained a second Guggenheim. He would continue to live in Washington even after he had thrown over official politics to be, not so much a poet, but a "writer." The stories were written with magazine publication in mind, perhaps even with the hope of payment. "Stocking Cap," for example, was sent to the *New Yorker* in February of 1948, where it received a prompt rejection (the notice in fact dated only three days after receipt of the story). "Mr. Meyer" was likewise rejected. While a note on the original manuscript of "The Post Office" indicates the story was either sent or considered for sending to the *Atlantic Monthly*, where Olson had published a poem, "Pacific Lament," two years earlier.

These reminiscences of his father were written almost three years after *Call Me Ishmael*, Olson's study of Melville, and shortly before Olson would break off his visits to Ezra Pound at St. Elizabeth's Hospital. Both Melville and Pound, it might be noted, were among the several self-acknowledged "fathers" in Olson's life. But the dedication of *Call Me Ishmael*, written in the language of a border ballad, was to his own father. Consciously antique, it is a poem of archaic tenderness: "O fahter, fahter / gone amoong / O eeys that loke / Loke, fahter: / your sone!" His father, who was born in Orebro, Sweden in 1882 and who had been carried to this country by his mother when he was a few months old, died in August of 1935 of a cerebral hemorrhage, shortly before his son would enter Harvard for graduate studies, joining the few other immigrant-sons such as Bernard DeVoto and Harry Levin. The inscription was thus his father's epitaph, and beside it, in his personal copy, Olson had pasted a photograph of him looking out into the sunlight. He had written an earlier poem in Key West around the time that Roosevelt died called "My Father," which began: "My father was my father / but my mother was the moon / She I have but he / died too soon."

His mother was born Mary Hines in Worcester in 1872, daughter of a family which had come from Ireland a few years before. It was in their frame house with a white picket fence around it on Middle River Road, later Mitchell Street, that Olson was born. She was a small woman, barely five feet tall, and a devout Catholic, keeping on her dresser a statue of Mother Mary. After her husband's death, she relocated permanently to Gloucester, breaking up house in Worcester and storing some of her possessions, including a dozen boxes of her son's books and papers, in the attic of her old friend, Mrs. Sullivan. The cottage she returned to in Gloucester was unheated, however, except by a fireplace made of pavingstones, and in the winters Mrs. Olson would seek shelter either in a boarding-house in Gloucester or with friends like the Sullivans in Worcester, in whose house she died on Christmas Day, 1950. Her son buried her in Worcester's Swedish Cemetery, alongside her husband.

The young Olson himself had been a substitute letter carrier in Gloucester for a few summers while on vacation from college, first on a route in the Fernwood section of West Gloucester, then in East Gloucester (where he would stop to talk to Susumu Hirota, a painter, and the Parenti sisters, as he tells us in *Maximus IV, V, VI*). An account of his appointment appeared in the *Gloucester Times* at the time, under the heading "Carrier Force Adds College 'Giant' to Fernwood Route." It begins: "Freeman D. Hodsdon, the 6 foot 2 mailman, has lost the honor of being the tallest man in the local department, for yesterday there was added to the force a young fellow by the name of George [sic] Olson, who unbends at 6 feet 6 inches. . . . He is probably the tallest mail carrier in the state, and tips the scales at 205 pounds. In fact, he was so high up in the air that as he complied with the regulation of having his fingerprints taken on his appointment, he was forced to get down on his knees to place his fingers on the fingerprint paper that lay on the table." One time, after he had assumed duties, his father secretly arranged it that he might appear unexpectedly in full uniform in Gloucester to help make the rounds with his son, to the delight of their friends and patrons.

Many years later, before he withdrew from party politics, Olson was informally offered, along with other possibilities, the post of Postmaster General in the Truman administration as a reward for his service to the Democratic National Committee by rallying foreign-language groups in support of the Party. He said he kicked himself afterwards for not having the quickness of mind to accept the position, if only for a single day, just long enough to avenge his father by punishing those men who had broken his father and who still held their posts in the post office in Worcester. He would have then resigned, with very great satisfaction, the next day!

These stories are all memories of Worcester, not Gloucester, and are set in the 1910s and 1920s in that city and its then still-rural environs, like Holden or Paxton, reachable by trolley—which the poet in *Maximus* calls his "inland waters." The time was "blueberry America"—a phrase he uses in his letter to Robert Creeley of March 8, 1951 and hints at in the *Maximus Poems*—a world that "went with the blueberries, / the chestnuts / with the openness the exploiters / had not beat out, was still walking, was going places / in street-cars." I pressed him once as to what world it was, this "blueberry America," and he said it as a definition: "That world waiting, when one could take a trolley to the city limits and walk in any direction and find blueberries to pick." It was a time before the suburbs, before the population explosion. But he would not stop there, with sentimentalism and a misty nostalgia; the passage from *Maximus* continues: "Not that the state of it / needs crying over. The real / is always worth the act of / lifting it, treading it / to be clear, to make it / clear . . ."

Olson had grown up in Worcester and came with his parents to Gloucester for summers only. The summer cottage, Oceanwood, with its hand-lettered driftwood sign, was rented from Homer Barrett, the former mayor of Gloucester, and Mrs. Olson in turn let out a few of its spare rooms to boarders. Her husband continued to work in the post office in Worcester, coming to the seashore only weekends, except for his fifteen-day vacation, arriving Friday night after work, when a supper would be waiting for him, and leaving at dawn on Monday morning in time to arrive for work. It was almost a three-hour ride on the interurban trolley.

The wooden "triple-decker" on Norman Avenue in south Worcester, in which the Olsons rented the top floor, still stands, although the once-open field behind it was filled in even during Olson's youth at the house. In that field—through which Beaver Brook passed, rusty even then from the junk in it, with its irises ("'flags' we called 'em") and a sudden turtle—was Fisher's Hill, where the young boy would imagine frontier redoubts out of Joseph Altsheler, whose books were so popular that the ten- and eleven-year old boys had to sign up on a waiting list at the public library for them, or bake potatoes with an imaginary playmate he had named Cabbage. His mother would summon him from the back porch with a whistle she kept hanging there for that purpose.

At the Berkeley Poetry Conference in 1965, after a moving reading and rediscovery of his poem "Ode on Nativity," Olson remarked: "Wow, I never wrote about Gloucester like this . . . I've been wrong all this time . . . I belong in, my subject is Worcester!" Had he forgotten? After reading these early, loving narratives, it is clear that at least one time before, it was.

George F. Butterick

* STOCKING CAP *

THE skill was not to snub the nose of the pickerel on the under edge of the ice as, with wet, numb hands, you brought him up—more often than not he was a perch—out of the water six inches or three feet down, as the winter went, from the frozen surface of the lake.

The rest was crude, cold work and my father saw to it that it began the moment we hit the ice, the sun hardly up. First, the cutting of the holes, round and eight to ten inches across, the only challenge that you not let go your grip, from stiff fingers, on the long, narrow steel of the chisel; the setting out of the tilts (like laths, but of a better wood, a foot and a half high) each in a slit chipped out close to the rim of a hole, with slush packed in to freeze it upright; the baiting of the lines and the rigging of them from each tilt, their fine thread sticking to the ice and hard to free with mittens on. Then, on shore, the gathering the wood and making the fire, the important thing the spot, protected but at some promontory from which all the tilts could be seen. And the rest of the day the ever repeating routine of the circuit of the holes, to skim them and to make sure that the wind or a nibble had not slipped the noose in the line off the tilt-arm that held it over the center of the hole.

It was this same arm, when a strike was a good one, which tripped and let go the red flannel flag and bent down on a spring from the top of the tilt, and it was these flags we gave our attention to, once the tilts were out, swigging coffee by the fire, always our eyes out over the surface of the lake to sight them, if and when one should go up, the exciting signal that started us on the run over the ice.

I suppose it was because my father picked his Sundays that way, but they all stand in my mind as sunny but wind-driven and bitter cold. I was allowed to bring my skates, though I could see he didn't much approve, it was not according to some Hoyle of ice fishing he had in his head. He made this exception of his son, however, and it gave the day a connection to other things one did in a New England winter. Otherwise it stood clear, stands clear now, as some glistening, cruel, attractive other country enclosed in dark, from the bitter dark of winter morning before dawn (when he waked me) to the travel home in the trolley at night and the sweet animal collapse the heat of the house and supper brought once we were back in the tenement, as though a blow had struck us, and we welcomed it, and went down under it, easily, pleasurably, back into sleep.

My father was a stickler for details and it seems now as though it was all week he was working on the gear although I suppose it was only the night before. This was a holiday, his chance to get free, and he treated it as he treated the other adventures he contrived for later seasons of the year; partridge berries, May flowers, elderberries for the wine he kept five years ahead, our trips to the dump for iron, his trips alone in summer to sketch for the water colors he did at nights at home. He fished at other times of the year but I never seem to have gone along, it was always some friend who went with him nights after work. He never caught any more than he did in the winter. The truth is, I don't think he cared. It was only another way of going free, getting out to the sensations of life. (I remember how irritated he was, when we went after walnuts once in the fall, because I did not see things as sharply or at the distance he did.)

And my weariness bothered him. Another ritual of the fall was grapes. He had found, how I could never figure out, wild vines of red and Concord grapes buried in a tangle of forest miles off the Boston-Worcester trolley line. We would set off circumspectly enough, with only a folded mail sack under his arm. The trolley ride was more than any train for me, rushing and wobbling as it did through mostly open country. The walk from the stop I remember as the high point next after that first sight of the grapes themselves. It was down a country road lined with apples, by farms and dogs and stock. My father was enough of a kid to stop, and gape, and dawdle as much as I did, throwing stones with me, hanging over a broken wall into a field, breaking off branches of trees along the road by hurling other rotted pieces at them like boomerangs.

It was when we started into the woods that I began to tire, and though the coming on the grapes was a tremendous thing, at which I marveled in my father, how he brought us to them, it wasn't long before I was plaguing him with questions, how long more we'd be and when we could go. I wonder now if it wasn't the presence of woods, they depress me so, even to this day. At first I was all right, the Concords tasted so good, and I gorged myself, eating more than I was putting in the sack. He'd laugh at me and tell me to get on with it, pick them not eat them, as he worked away raking them from the vines into the bag. But it was when we had all those within easy reach and it was necessary for him to climb the tree to follow the vine as it wound itself upward and I was left alone below with the woods that I'd begin to complain and he must have thought I sounded like my mother.

I don't remember much the road back but I do remember the wonderful stains on the sack, and the care we had to keep it away from our clothes and a self-consciousness when we were back in the city and stood on the rear platform of the trolleys with our bag.

Only once in winter, strangely enough, do I seem to have been inadequate, and that time, I think, he was complaining for the show of it, and to set himself a little bit above my mother. It was the time my two cousins, older than I, came with us. It was a severe day, the temperature below zero, and when we left the house my mother made a scene against his taking me. "You'll kill him," she said; "you'll be the death of him." It was a tough day, and I dare say I did feel the cold, but I was determined to go, and I put up with his jibes before my cousins, for even then I sensed they were meant for my mother, and not for me. They were compliments, in a way, for I was along, and they called my cousins' attention to that fact, and that he had a son who could stay with them.

His main concern each of those winter trips was the chisel. The tilts took care of themselves. They came home ready for use again no matter how cold or dark it had been when we had left the lake the previous time. He would never allow them to be wound carelessly as I have seen other fishermen do. But the chisel always needed new attention. It was one he had made himself. (I remember how surprised and scornful I was when I discovered, once we fished a large lake nearer the city, that other men had wider, store-bought chisels and that they called them by another name.) His was arranged in sections, out of pipe, in lengths about as long as tilts so that all our gear could be strapped together in a bundle. The threaded sleeves of the sections fascinated me, and the putting of them together, but the important part to him was the cutting end. It was no thicker or wider than a tilt and may have been his own design. It was this he sharpened with such care.

I was puzzled he took no more than one along. I suppose it was weight that dictated but I knew they could get lost, slip out of a cold hand and when you suddenly broke through that last plug of ice, and the water came up, and sloshed over your feet. He had lost one once, and I think I did, and once we were able to fish one out of shallow water, how I can't now say. The curious thing was I don't think he ever had a rope on the chisel's end as other men had and as you'd think he might. Perhaps it was another of those queer obstacles he had a way of dealing with as a challenge and which made him such an attractive, tragic man. The stubborn side of it killed him in the end.

The bait pail and the skimmer were the other crucial tools. Only once do I remember getting the minnows the day we fished—from a little old man in a shanty on the way, a professional, I thought, compared to us. The other times, I suppose, my father brought the minnows home from work, for he was careful with them, to keep the water right and to leave them out on the back porch over night. On the way to the lake they had to be carried most carefully, not to jounce, and to be looked at several times on the ride to make sure they did not die. Always one or two did, and to see them turned up, lolling in the water, sickened me. It wasn't the same when they were dead from being on the hook too long in the holes. The holes, before the day was through, were circled with them, side up, with big eyes, frozen in the ice.

The advance to the lake was always new, as sharp as I imagine the discovery of a continent used to be—the whiteness, the curiosity whether anyone else might be there first (then I was always so overwhelmed with disappointment I wanted to go home), the rush to start the holes, the decisions how to lay them, the question, how thick the ice. I suppose the work of cutting was inviting for its warmth but it was exhausting and I was interested, long before my father would allow himself to be, in the fire.

The fire was, for me, the big business of the day. With the lines out the fishing depended on the fish, but the fire, that depended on me. I fetched the wood and started it. I kept it alive. I tore my mittens feeding it. I burned my coat hugging it, I had to stand so close to keep warm I was forever sure my rubbers would crack or melt away. Or the wind would gust, and scatter the fire, and I'd have to go off farther and farther into the woods to get new wood for it and lose a mitten doing it, and come back with snow-bit hands.

But it was home, and everything centered on it, and

though it always arranged to tip the coffee pot into itself, and burn the handle so I'd burn myself righting it, the fire was a precious thing and I was proud of its care, and built lives around it. (Most of the time it became a fort in which I barricaded myself against the woods, and the lake was a plain I scanned vigilantly—as though it might hide Indians as well as red topped tilts.)

It was also, of course, the place you came back gladly to from the ice, from a run out to play a fish or to patrol the nearer holes. And food had a special taste because of it, covered with soot from the tending of it, seasoned with the smell of each of the trees we were using for it, and the smoke entering the mouth with each bite as much as the meat.

So I was the guard, the mother of the fire, while my father, ever active, kept restlessly touring the ice, hoping a flag would go up, changing the tilts, cutting new holes to find the fishes' feeding ground. And sometimes he'd go off around some headland of the lake and be gone so long I'd get nervous and strike out after him. Or at least go far enough to get a better look-out for him without losing sight of the tilts. For it was always my hope, when he went off like that, that a flag would go up and all by myself I would land the biggest pickerel of the day.

It was the dying of the day on those lakes which gave me my first taste, I suppose, of wan-hope. No matter what I did the fire seemed to go down as the sun did, and when that light which comes as brightness goes off and that cold which settles as the wind dies would spread in from the lake, I first knew some secret of death.

It was an attractive hour. My father's figure out on the ice grew and his stocking cap became the fur crown of some Siberian trader. His overcoat filled out and though I knew it was green with age, and torn, it was fur too, and he was grand. His run, always peculiar from his thick-soled rubbers and his layers of clothes, was now immense.

The tilts were easier to see and though the flags flew up less often—they never kept us busy enough—they were startling when they did and my shout, or my father's run, was sharp like teeth on the grey ice and in the blue air. This was one of the times when I shared my father's feelings precisely: I was as prepared as he to linger as the day ran out. He stayed, perhaps, because he hoped for one more fish.

It is wood smoke that always throws me back to those wild days, the stain of it, sweet and sharp and green, in our stocking caps and hair, in our eyes and clothes (more than the dye of them), and in my nose and mouth and mind as we stepped into that welcome thing, the trolley car, to set off for home.

* MR. MEYER *

THERE was a tailor named Meyer who fixed my father's clothes, a short, warm, round man of whom I was most fond. My father was a letter carrier and his uniforms were constantly in need of patching, particularly on the shoulder where the bag was carried and along the side of the coat where the bottom of the bag wore the cloth away.

My father had left his trade as an iron worker some time before I was born. At that time, before the first world war, the salary of a letter carrier was higher and offered the flypaper that even the best of the lower middle class get caught on, security.

During that war and after, when other salaries went up, my father had lost the gain and was left only with the security, and that of the lowest, meanest kind. So uniforms, which the postmen had to buy for themselves, had to be made to last until there was little left of the original garment. My mother, I know, kept up with them as well as she could, repairing and relining, using the old to reinforce the new, working a season ahead, the heavier winter things at her machine in the fall, the spring and summer stuff as the winter began to ease off.

But there were certain jobs, like the shoulder patch, which took a tailor's skill, and that, I guess, was when Mr. Meyer came in. I imagine he did such work for other carriers and it was through them my father learned of him although vaguely, in the back of my mind, are some broken pieces of a memory that it was in answer to an advertisement of Mr. Meyer's that my father got in touch with him.

I know one thing. He lived at the other end of the city on a street the name of which is so joined to him I can never separate them. It was Burncoat Street.

It only strikes me now why that name obviously settled into my subconscious joined to Mr. Meyer. I had previously thought it was fastened there because of one winter night when, for some reason, Mr. Meyer could not come across the city to us, as was the custom, to pick up the clothes or to do some work, and my father and I had to go over on the streetcars to his shop.

It may have been the hour and the weather, or perhaps it was because I was thus up later than usual, but it was probably the intensity of the sight of him, small as he was, bent over his table with the only light in the shop the green shade above his head (the shadows peopled with uncertain figures called coats and the floor and tables ambushes of pants and dresses). It opened up a whole new side of him for me, the professional I had not the experience to recognize in him as I had come to know him in our home.

He used to come over carrying a paper bag, and sweating, not, I felt, from hurrying so much as from the working of that quality which marked him for me, his shyness. I was aware that other people were shy but whether I knew it then I know now their shyness was brittle. It was not how they were in their natures but how people took them, a social matter which didn't go any deeper than their vanities. I could sense that when they went away and talked to someone they felt superior to, or when they were alone, they were able to justify themselves, shoring up the details which tore the enemy, that other human being they were not sure of, down. The thing was not so much shyness as narrowness. There was no modesty in it.

It was the modesty of Mr. Meyer which lay at the bottom of the motions of his character. Though he was inordinately shy and seemed to want to stay in a smaller, more inconspicuous place than he occupied in a room or on a streetcar, he was not withdrawn, hunched up within some silly fear without reference to either animal or human life. There was in fact a very strong animal quality about him, wrapped up in his rusty and black clothes. His flesh was fat and his very white skin was not dry like most of the people I knew, and his eyes, which moved more than other people's, were bare and beautiful and I could look at them only in snatches.

Now that I come to think of it I wonder if Meyer was

not his first name and that I called him Mr. Meyer out of my great respect and love for him. I think, too, that what he carried in his paper bag was food, so that he would not be a burden on my mother. For there was an attitude of not wishing to impose on anyone, which went with him and which he carried faultlessly. He came to work, and he did his work without spreading himself outside its limits. It was a very strong thing.

My father, however, who was more sure of himself (and less sure) than Mr. Meyer, would lead him out, tease him (as he had a way of doing with others) on the surfaces of his personality. It was a talent, I suppose you might say, of my father, though it made me very nervous, and saddened me, for I knew its other side. There was a party once of the "campers," as they called themselves, who had a group of houses in the summer built in an old settlement near the sea. It was an anniversary of their coming there, the fifth maybe, for there is a picture of them, in costumes and out, posed against the house in back of ours. My mother is there in a white dress and with her black hair combed in a pompadour (as it is in the picture of her at the time of her marriage), and my father with his big face and his arm slung around some woman, and myself on the roof with my stockinged legs dangling down. It must have been about when I was ten. Anyhow, the climax of the celebration was a minstrel show in our camp and it is the impression my father made which first sharpened my attention to that side of him which made people use the word "fun." It wasn't so much what he did that I remember as a curtain with sunflowers painted on it. Holes were cut out where the blossoms were and each of the men were posed behind it with their heads through. And the faces that my father made! And the antics!

He had a way of being liked, for his energy. He'd sing and dance and play tricks, get up fishing parties or walks. There was a bravura about it, a hectic note which I could only put up with because I had seen the other thing, the sudden distaste, or sombreness, the sense of the effort wasted. For he was awkward, unable to cope with the failings of life except by himself, in his early morning walks, fishing, painting, or carpentry, when he could bear down and get his restless flying off from the nubs of life concentrated.

He did not have what Mr. Meyer had, what maybe any tailor has, that squatting with life over a needle. In any case Mr. Meyer had it, and I think my father knew, for there was a good deal of affection between them. My father was a big man and to see Mr. Meyer smiling and talking up to him, and my father, with his broader style, haggling with Mr. Meyer, was a pleasure for me.

It was as though Mr. Meyer was closer to older roots of life, and my father, who had been here since he was three months old, had gotten so far away from them he had almost lost them. Yet he had the need, as we all do, for them, and Mr. Meyer pulled him back. I can think of only one other man who did something similar for him, and he was a little man too, but it was of another order of feeling, and is another story.

Mr. Meyer had a family but I don't know that we ever saw them, even that night we went to his shop. My mother and my father always asked after them, and I recall there were clothes given to him, for he was poor, and there were several kids. It seems, too, that my mother sent candy with him, her fudge, I suppose. I hated to have him go and I would run around to the front window (we were three stories up) to see him again as he emerged into the street and to watch his figure in the street lights. He caught the trolley at the corner. Sometimes I could see him get in. It gave me as deep a feeling as I have ever known of man and his naturally accumulated, fated responsibilities.

Charles Olson, Sr., *ca.* 1934; courtesy the Olson Archives.

The Olson family at Stage Fort Park, Gloucester, *ca.* 1918; courtesy Constance Bunker.

Olson around sixteen years old, with parents in front of Oceanwood Cottage, Gloucester; courtesy the Olson Archives.

The two mailmen, courtesy the Olson Archives.

A trolley of the Boston & Worcester Street Railway, the "Trolley Air Line," at a stop in Wellesley Hills, Mass., where Olson would go as a boy with his father to visit his Aunt Vandla. Photo from the collection of George King, Jr.

* THE POST OFFICE *

I SAID it was my father's stubbornness that killed him in the end. It was, and the trouble out of which his death came was born fourteen years earlier. In its birth he was right. The fight he put up was a just one.

I can date it that exactly because it was his determination to take me to the celebration at Plymouth of the 300th anniversary of the Pilgrim landing that aggravated the situation his superiors in the Post Office had provoked.

My father had requested and received permission to take his vacation the week of the pageant at Plymouth. He and I were to go, leaving my mother at home. It was to be our first big trip and he had planned it most carefully, for it was a major excursion for him as well, comparable only to his trip alone, before I was born, to Gettysburg.

That trip had also got him into trouble, but of another

sort, less mortal. It was with my mother. As far as I could ever get the picture he surprised her by going off, so soon after their marriage, on a holiday of his own. This may be a little unfair to her. It may be that the running references to the trip that I heard the rest of the years my father was alive were nothing more than the taunts by which we remind ourselves as well as the other of experience we have not shared. It is a part of that play of jealousy which inhabits the intimate life as much as affection does.

I myself was satisfied with the trip as was, as I heard it from him and as I was reminded of it by the two small pitchers he had brought back for my mother, of a most delicate porcelain, with scenes on them. They set on the mantelpiece in the dining-room and erased for me the two hideous vases at each end of the shelf, fat cylinders of unglazed flowered glass which looked to me as ugly as legs without ankles. In fact I was so delighted in my father's taste in choosing the pitchers that they created in me a delight in the trip which makes it more sweet in memory than any of my own.

But not my mother. His letters or the pitchers or her sure sense the trip was right for him precisely as it had been made never blotted out what also stood on the shelf of her mind. It never does. She had the greed we have, to know all that happens to the other person. Our imagination won't, in this circumstance, stay straight. It corrupts, and we go back and back, as greedy to know as we are fearful to know too much.

Maybe my mother made so much of their marriage trip to New York to offset this Gettysburg which followed hard on it. They arrived in a blizzard and stayed at the old Grand Central Hotel. One thing stood out that could be talked about and that my mother dwelt on with a blush. She had packed no button hook for her high shoes. My father had to go out in the storm and at that hour find some store open. He picked up their umbrella, one of the wedding presents, and when he stepped out into the snow he stepped, she delighted to put it, into a rice storm as well!

I was not ten when the Plymouth trip was planned but my father had long since got over to me his interest in the American past. Any boy brought up in New England had worn the high hat and square, buckled shoes at Thanksgiving plays at school and written a life of George Washington round and round an elm tree at Cambridge. My father had taken me several steps down from that.

I'm not sure his first service wasn't on the biography of General George. I was working on it at the kitchen table with my mother ironing by the stove and him across from me over a drawing board, probably finishing a black and white (he was at that time making up for the schooling he didn't get by shipping lessons to a correspondence institute of art in Minneapolis). The essay was too much for me and I suddenly threw it up in disgust.

The gesture struck him with almost the same force as the dice of the parchesi box did the time I dished them into his face in my anger he had licked me. That time he chased me and would have whaled me had it not been for my mother's frantic fear. When he caught up with me by the set tubs he contented himself with a milder torture. He merely pulled my hair.

Over George Washington he was gentle and strong. He talked. And he made his point, the more easily, I suppose, because I knew how thoroughly he himself worked, over a drawing board or on our neighbors' boilers or their plumbing. I had already learned one trick from him, handing tools to him: you can swear your way through the dirtiest weather. As his assistant then I acquired almost as good a tongue as I was later to, from certain fishermen I know.

What he had to say about me and George Washington was: do it. And I did it. It took.

It is easy to figure out how old I was. The paper was read to the class but I was completely embarrassed, especially because of Margarite Luddon who had the seat in front of me, and such beeyootiful hair. All the "of's," the teacher wanted the class to know, and there must be a lot of them in a biography, were spelt "uv"!

It was the Matthew Bradys my father gave me as a child that have influenced my sense of the past to this day. I have the set. It was the *Review of Reviews* issue of the *Photographic History.* They came, by subscription,

I suppose, as thin, large, blue paperbound pamphlets which I could lay open page by page on the floor. The photographs cured me that early of romantic history. I preferred Brady to the colored frontispiece each one carried of some fool's oil on Grant at Lookout Mt or Burnside at Nashville. I could take that as narrative in Joseph Altsheler, *The Rock of Chickamauga*, say. Or in the annual play my father made it a ritual to take me to, even though, each year I ducked behind the back of the seat in front of me when the volley came which cut the hero down. It was year after year, one play, "The Drummer Boy of Shiloh."

Once Brady had taught my eyes, I broke through the painted surfaces of war. The dead in Devil's Gulch at Gettysburg, this was something I was not shown at school. Or horses puffed up on a field huge beside the corpses of men or humped in a ditch along some Wilderness road. Or those groups of Brady's, men and women standing with the curiously penetrating eyes Brady's wet plate seemed to fix, at a distance though he was, focussed down on some Virginia "Station" through a grove of stripped trees. These, too, school did not give me.

Or my father, for that matter. I wonder now what Brady did for him. Maybe, just because I was born here, I had the jump on him. He valued America, as immigrants do, more than the native. I'm not sure it's a good thing. It wasn't, in my father's case, as this trouble he got himself into will show, though for me his fascination with the story of this country was fruitful, as it sometimes is, in the second generation American. There is a sentimentality about the freedoms of this country which none of the bitterness of poverty and abuse will shake in an immigrant. My father had it, at least up to this trouble I write about when the government of these States so failed him he was thrown back on that other rock of the immigrant, his foreign nationality organizations.

It took something out of my father's historical soul. From then on he localized his interest to the past of Gloucester and the fishing industry. That, I think, was a gain and, had he lived, it would have given his life and his painting a ground. That was a more usable, economic America than the society of the rights of man which failed him.

But he did something else, which was not helpful. To some degree he substituted Sweden for America as a focus for his curiosity, after the "Americans" failed him in his fight and he had to turn to the Swedish-American societies for aid. They are like mothers anyway, these societies, keeping their children back from the brunt of this country. They aid them but they also fondle them when they are hurt or cut to pieces as they so often are on the steel points of the society.

I think there can be no doubt my father let down and accepted some of this caressing from 1920 on. Nor can I blame him, for he was gravely wounded. I only have this feeling. If he had lived (he was only 52 when he died) I think there was a good chance, given his intelligence and a couple of N.A.L.C. victories he was on the point of winning, that he might have mended. With the help of Gloucester, he might have seen his struggle outside both Sweden and America, as a part of this ambiguous battle all human society is now, for good or evil, engaged in.

It was something of this view that I was trying to give him in his last years, a meagre return for the childhood he gave me. I argued that, if he were to pitch his energies true, he needed to free himself from the narrow area of recrimination into which the enemy had maneuvered him. But I am ahead of my story. Let me say this: I carried one thing home from Plymouth, the broken shaft of an arrow. I found it on the ground behind the stage after the pageant was over.

I better spell the situation out. Postal employees do not have the right to strike. The result is, union organization among carriers and clerks has lagged. On top of that their organizations have tended, because their officers must wheedle and act mostly as lobbyists on Congress, to continue the same men in national office for unhealthy periods of time. The upshot is, the rank and file are about as spiritless a group of workers as you can imagine and their officers have more in common with the Post Office officials than with the men they represent.

This was hardly a condition a fighter like my father could abide. I can't say where he first acquired his sense of workingmen's rights. I think it was more a matter of his bones than training. He had gone to work at fourteen to aid his mother in the support of himself and two sisters. He had a milk route.

He was one of those men for whom newspapers are education. The few times I saw him with a book in his hands he struck me as most awkward, and he soon fell asleep. (The only exception was a complete one. It was *Handy-Andy*. He read it to me nights while I recovered from a tonsil and adenoid operation. I have never, in anyone else's hands, seen a book do like convulsive things.)

I don't even have the impression that his employment as an iron worker, before he became a letter carrier, contributed to him, in any direct way, as a labor organizer. He stayed with the same firm in which he learned the trade, and it was a family business, and a small shop. My father was, in fact, the leader of a crew of master builders. The work of the firm (it was the Stewart Boiler Works) was principally the raising, all over New England, of those huge factory stacks which replaced brick in the expanding days of industry at the turn of the century. For some reason Calais, Maine (I heard it "callous") came to be the place where I put him when I imagined him high on a staging setting the final lip to the chimney. To this day I can't quite get over the difficulty I then had to figure out how he got down. I could only imagine the descent as made down through the long hole of the completed chimney, and it gave me then, and gives me now, whatever is the inside out of vertigo. It was an exciting thing, this image of him, as a man of heights, and was, I suppose, as satisfying a way as a son can see his father.

Calais, by the way, got chosen, I'm sure, because it looked and sounded strange enough to be a frontier and fitted the map my mind made of the wanderings of this hero of mine as I had constructed it from the tales I picked up. It was a part of the satisfaction I drew from this employment, that it led my father to all sorts of unknown lands and continents in Rhode Island, Massachusetts, New Hampshire and Maine. Calais was Gades, the farthest outpost. It was from Calais, I think, that he proposed to my mother. There was some important business attached to it. Perhaps it was the Canadian stamps on the postcards he sent to her from the town across the river from Calais.

Whatever organizing he had done in his fourteen years in the Post Office before 1920, it was that blow-off which first made me aware that carrying mail involved my father in other things than going away in the morning and returning at night. I knew that occasionally he would go out in the evenings, to what were called "meetings." But so far as I was concerned the day reached a climax when he came home from work as the afternoon fell off. I had a habit of waiting for him at the head of the street. (Later it was to watch for him as we played ball in the field which stretched from our backyard as far as Hill's barn. We used to get him to come and knock flies out to us before we'd let him go upstairs.) He was a gay man and I guess I first knew how gay he was the night he came home with what they then called an ulcerated tooth. When I met him and he walked me down the street without a word or greeting I fell into step beside him as troubled as he. His face was so held and his walk so careful I was completely bewildered. I did not dare to look at him more than once or twice. That night the street was very long. It was the first time, I suppose, that I went along a sidewalk in that blind way which causes time and space to distend. Once we were home I had to go out to get flaxseed poultice but he continued to suffer so, the house that night stayed like the street. It was never his teeth again, but from 1920 on he was more often grim, when I met him, than gay.

What happened was this: the postmaster cancelled his vacation the night before we were to leave. It was a most unusual act, and all that I was ever able to find out confirms the fact they did it because my father was the wheelhorse of the union and they wanted, in this small way, to get back at him.

I don't know that they knew he'd play into their hands as he did. The foreman of carriers, Paddy Hehir (hair, the Irish pronounce it), knew my father, and my mother, well. It could be that he knew, and passed on, how much this trip was in my father's mind. But I think not. Paddy's part was otherwise. I'm inclined to believe the bosses didn't know. I'm inclined to think they just decided to balk my father for no other reason than a vacation gave them a chance.

It was Blocky Sheehan, as they called him, the Superintendent of Mails, whom my father, to the end of his life, blamed for the whole business. And Sheehan could only have known the special point of the trip from Paddy or another carrier. As I say, I doubt it was that plotted.

It was the fact that Sheehan and the Postmaster had first granted him permission that forever after was the stake to which my father was tied. It was the injustice of it, the dirty, underhanded trick, I seem to hear him say. He had made Branch 12 of the N.A.L.C. (National Association of Letter Carriers) strong, for the first time, I believe. That was enough. But he was also in correspondence with the State officers of the union and he had already, if my memory is correct, been active in pushing, through the Branch and the annual convention of the N.A.L.C., such programs as national legislation in favor of thirty year optional retirement, the widows' pension, and other like long-range goals. He was a "trouble-maker." He and his pal, Dinny Riordan, who had had legal training nights before he became a carrier, were too active for the bosses, too smart, and they figured this was the time to set my father back.

It did, but not the way they thought. He didn't take it. We went off the next morning as planned.

I knew nothing about the trouble of course and to this day I can remember nothing in my father's behaviour that whole week which gave me any clue that there was anything wrong. He did everything to the hilt, as usual. We missed nothing and I still have a sight of one moment of his face as some costume or float or incident in the parade pleased him and I noticed his sudden pleasure, and the way his hair blew. He had taken his hat off, that flat, stiff straw he wore each summer, the old kind with broad straw woven like fish scales, and it had left a red mark on his forehead near the hair, and I noticed it, and beads of sweat.

We saw the pageant night after night. We went aboard the model of the *Mayflower*. We found the old cemetery pitched up over the town. We went out to Duxbury, to Miles Standish and Priscilla Alden's graves. We visited the Plymouth Cordage Company. At least he did. For it seems to me it was there I met him after my Sunday morning venture which became one of those standing jokes in the family.

My mother was a Catholic and I was raised one. The problem was, in Plymouth, where I'd go to mass. Somewhere around the Cordage Co. we found a church my father and I decided must be Catholic. It had the right cross on it, I guess. I went in and he went on, to look over ropes. It wasn't very long when I was out, and so confused to be out so quickly I could not tell him, any more than I could my mother afterwards, that I was sure I had been to a Catholic service. I knew only one thing, that when I had entered handbells were ringing as they are, in the mass, when communion is being prepared. I was sure this at least would satisfy my mother but, on the contrary, it made her only the more upset, for if it were that long after the Gospel that you went in, said she, with a voice that sounded as though she were wringing her hands, you did not hear Mass at all!

For my father the irony of that week must have been that the family we stayed with was that of the Postmaster of North Plymouth! It was one of those gentle houses the New Englanders of the 17th century built and the pleasure of it, of the trees at Duxbury and the sea at Plymouth meant more to me (at least I am stained more with the traces) than the excitements we had come to Plymouth to enjoy. The Postmaster was a Mr. Brown. My father had met him at some convention and it is a measure of how much my father's heart was set on this trip that he had arranged our room with Mr. Brown ahead of time.

It was not like him. I take that from him. He much preferred to set off, recklessly sure that things would work out in their courses. (It was that way the only time we were in New York together. He ended up sharing my hotel room. And forgot his straight edge razor when we left in the morning and only remembered it when we were home. Which worried him, for it was his pride, and he honed it stroke after stroke, wiping the lather off on pieces of toilet paper. He wasn't sure he'd get it back, for we'd left the registration single, to save money, when he had failed to find a room for himself and had come to bunk with me.)

The week passed, and what happened when we returned, so sharply changed life in my home that that week came to mean the end of my childhood. Up to then there had been a cocoon of peace and ease around my nerves. It was so pure it was amniotic, and has left me, it has been my thought, those several years retarded. They multiplied security, my mother and my father were so balanced, and when the change came it tore a fabric so delicate it just blew away.

It is also my thought that, because it was my father who was struck, intensified the role he played for me before and after. He had an added dimension because he was the single image of life, I had lived so long in the sleep of the mother.

They busted him, for insubordination and profanity. It seems he had called Paddy Hehir a son of a bitch when Paddy told him his vacation had been revoked. On top of that, of course, he had done the undoable, when he had up and gone without permission. That was insubordination to duty, to the Postmaster, to the President, to God.

There was only one larger crime, to rob the mails.

They had my father, and they didn't let go. The postal system has resemblances to the Army. There is, for example, a demerit system. The offenses are graduated and, in their degree, a man's pay is docked. They gave my father the maximum, and our scale of living, poor as it was, went down.

But they didn't stop there. They did the one thing which in those days would cut a veteran letter carrier to the heart. They took my father off his route. Men worked for years to get the routes they wanted. The routes would open as older men retired and the carriers bid for them, by seniority, in turn. Each man had his sense of the kind of route and what part of the city he liked best and this process of selection tended to make both the carrier and the people he served congenial.

For years my father had had the route he wanted. It stretched along the lake which bounds the city on the east. Originally the route ran on both sides of the lake south from the bridge which carried the road to Boston. The bridge alone, and the other wooded side (where nothing much was but the city's amusement park and some summer camps) were enough to make the route what my father would like. Just to cross the bridge a winter morning and a winter afternoon, or to be a part of the boating around it in the summer and the fall, gave his work day a freedom he could never have known in any other route in the city. The whole route had this quality. On the city side it was a series of streets, "avenues" most of them were called, running parallel to the lake, each a little higher up the gradual slope from it, on which people of small means had built mostly one and a half story homes around the turn of the century. They had left room between themselves and their neighbors and the route was a walker, appropriate to a man with my father's legs and drive. Dogs, for example, ran free and, for some strange reason, attached themselves to him in troupes. (They usually dislike carriers, for the straps they carry, and the way the bag swings when it is unslung from the shoulder. Or so I found when I was a carrier later. They'd come through a screen door to get me in the leg.) My father had so many stories about them that I remember their names and the differences of their natures better than I do most of the people who owned them. He had his favorites for years, who went the whole route with him and who became as well known as he was, along the way. He'd set them off against each other yet see that the butchers in the stores at the corners had meat for them. When one Airedale, Cuppy, was killed by the trolley which ran to the lake down a freeway which cut through the backyards of the settlement, my father was disconsolate for days. There is a picture of him, in a new uniform, with Cuppy pawing him to the shoulders like some mythic lion.

And then there was the life directly on the lake to give the route a fillip a residential area never has. There was the Lincoln Park Theatre on this side of the bridge, to which I was taken on passes in the summer evenings down the freeway in the open cars. And the Chinese who had a wheel concession near the theatre on the Boston road, who each year gave my father, for my mother, some new set of china. (They came packed in a fine straw which interested me.) And the boathouses directly on the lake. Randall's was my father's favorite, or, rather, he was a favorite of the Randalls. Sundays, when the ice was gone, he would take me to Randall's and we would go out together on the lake after a lot of talk between him and the Randall boys during which time I gawked at the racing shells and the canoes set on racks up to the ceiling. And, towards the end of the route south, where the settlement ran off into the woods (in which the city had placed the little herd of what looked to me like moth-eaten buffaloes), was the ice house. My father got me a job there one Christmas vacation when I was in high school and it should have made a man of me. I cut ice with the men from 6 in the morning until 6 at night, and the only thing I can say for the day was, that I waited in terror, for my father's appearance, in the middle of the morning and the afternoon, when he was sure to hail me from the shore and make fun to the men of the way I poled the cakes through the channel into the elevator incline which took the ice up three flights to the house for storing.

Of the people, Martin and Minnie Hester seem to have

been the oldest, most continuous friends my father had. I remember the upset when Mr. Hester died. I think he was a carpenter, though I may have this confused with Martin and Nora Reidy. She was my godmother, and Martin was a carpenter in the city school system. Nora marked my birthdays. She always gave me gloves, and was the only one outside the family who remembered my birthday. It fell two days after Christmas. But Martin studded my school days. It was unexpected and delightful to have him turn up at my grammar school. Later, when I was in high school and worked as the cashier at the lunch counter, I saw a lot of him. He used to come over and eat his lunch with me as I sold the tickets. Whenever the Hesters were mentioned it was the life of the Reidys, which I knew intimately (they were brother and sister, both unmarried), that rose up in my mind. I still have to work it out to realize that the Hesters were not a bachelor and an old maid. They remembered my father every Christmas and when he was off the route were most solicitous, though I don't think they played any part in organizing the protest of the people of the route against the Post Office officials. They were too shy.

That was the doing of men like Mr. Lawrence. He had a print shop, and I may remember him more, because he also invented a solution to soften typewriter rollers, and there were a few Saturdays, very few, when I, at my father's urging, made the rounds of the factories in our neighborhood trying to sell the stuff to secretaries and office managers. It was as dreadful to me as another attempt, to sell Mr. Lawrence's letter paper, with the name done to order. (The only time door to door selling interested me was Christmas cards, for the Waltham Company, and that took no selling, and gave me a huge profit, 50¢ on a dollar box.) But Mr. Lawrence stands in my mind as one of the leaders who called the several meetings at the Lake, as we called the route, to take action to get my father back.

I recall the Biancis, mostly for the huge Italian dinner, my first spaghetti and meatballs, that we and the Foleys were invited to. I have the feeling they were on Pat Foley's route, which joined my father's on the city side.

Most of the other names are gone. There were the Siskins, who had the meat market, and who spoiled my father's dogs. But the others, though remnants of my father's talk about them swim in my mind, have lost their faces and their names. There was an Irish girl who kept house for the priests, and it was one of my father's favorite diversions to plague her with his skepticisms about religion when he knew that one of the curates was listening in the next room. Once, with great care, he decorated and wrapped a brick as a fool's present for her, in lieu of what object she wanted I can't say. He was given to wrapping and boxing minute presents in huge boxes which he had the parcel post carrier deliver with extra fanfare. This seems to have been a part of the give and take of the route. He came home once with a box of fool's candy, soft ones of pepper, nougats of tobacco, thin ones of cardboard. He had been taken in and tried them on us.

I imagine the ones I have remembered are those with whom I had something to do. The vast majority I never saw, even though on one grand occasion I went the route with my father. I must have been about twelve. I don't know what the occasion was, but I do recall the place that impressed me most. It was the State Insane Hospital. It occupied the whole of the hill to the lake on the opposite side of the Boston road from the body of my father's route. The buildings, brownstone and like a college, were at the top and the farm ran down the slope behind a fence which seems to me now to have been made of rails, though it probably was of stone. It was along this fence that the inmates sat or walked, and their eyes, clothes, postures and gestures were a world of people I found much more interesting than the rest of us. From that day on, whenever I would go to the Lake of a Sunday or could get my father to talk, it was these men I wanted to see and hear of. They got mixed up in my mind with Brady's people of the Civil War. When I was told that the Reidys' sister Agnes had died in that hospital I could not bring the fact together with the fable the men along the fence stood for. (I even had some of the same difficulty much, much later when Martin Reidy was taken there. It was after my mother had lived with them, the winter following my father's death. I had visited with them at Christmas and though there was a difference in Nora and Martin

[Nora had always made me nervous ever since the hate she showed in arguments with my father over the Germans during the first world war] I attributed it to age. The house still smelled of Martin's good tobacco and was as remarkably neat as Nora had always kept it. No one was prepared for the crisis when it came. One night Nora waked to find Martin going around the house with an axe, looking under all the beds and accusing her of intimate relations with their nephew who lived upstairs.) Some of the nuts, as they were called, were free to leave the grounds and used to walk my father's route with him. One carved things as presents for him. My father gave them smokes and clothes.

That route was my father's parish, village to which he was crier and walking mayor. He was more intimate to the community, and the lives of all the people, than anyone else could be. The people showed it, the way they fought for him, when the crisis came.

Some of it was himself but part the fact he was "the postman." Mail, over any length of time, will tell secrets a neighbor could not guess. Nor do I mean the reading of postcards or the "lamping" of letters. Nor what a man hears over coffee. Or that a man's mail does not always come to his house, or a woman's either. It lies more in the manner in which people look for, ask for, receive their mail. And talk about it.

A letter, expected or surprise, is a lance, and the vizor slips, and I talk to this person to get it back into place, for I know him every day and yet I do not know him so well a confidence will lead me anywhere. I am aware I am vulnerable and I will regret a little some of the things I am saying, but . . . the uniform makes Mr. Olson anonymous enough.

This was most true in the days before Burleson, Wilson's Postmaster General, took the craft and country quality out of the service. The loss was the loss common to most labor since. This better be understood as not nostalgia. I was a letter carrier myself later and do not hark back. We have got so used to change that we are unwilling to believe that suddenly some change may be so total as to destroy. The path does die, and there are times when, to find his way back, man has to pick up, fiercely and without any easy emotion, traces of the way. What happened to work during the first world war is a trace.

Carrying mail never did require great skill any more than most of the broad-gauged jobs which make society run. You have heard all either of us wants to hear of the carrier the Man of Weather—sleet snow night rain: excelsior. What is not mentioned are hernia rheumatism flatfeet death (insurance company average) 52. The hazards. I can add, of Charles Olson Sr., (1) a fall down a flight of 30 stone steps & like incidents in the line of duty, (2) the morning he was brought home, before I had left for school, to my mother's and my surprise—a trolley car had split a switch and spread him out full six foot three on the pavement at Front and

Pleasant Streets. This kind of weather lasts.

What can be lost is the weather of a man. What gave the carrier dignity, the sense of accomplishment, what made his day of use to the people he served as well as to himself was the illusion that how he did it was of value.

Here is the connection between Burleson and what the bosses did to my father. My father did not want union power. He never held or sought top office. He served some terms as secretary, but not to control from that powerful post. To get the work done. For several years I did his typing and can say. What he was after, what all the legislation he pushed was directed against, was the speed-up. I used to get pretty bored with figures on the occupational diseases of letter carriers, calculations on the differentials of the volume of mail over a month, statistics on the condition of the widows of carriers, numbers of children per family etc., but it is clear that he saw what the fight was.

I'm sure the bosses were too knowing to think he could take the union over. He did not have that will and if he had they knew how to buy such men off. In some awkward way, with no scheme or large sense of what was involved, out of the needs of his own personality, his assurance that the satisfaction of a job lay in the perfection of the doing of it, the pounding of a rivet, the use of pumice after sandpaper to make a surface ready for a stain, the fixative to set a crayon sketch for O. Victor Humann at the Museum, led my father to fight for quality against efficiency in the postal service. That was, and is, the battle-line.

He was the resistance of a man, my father, the cry of the individual that he be allowed the time and the conditions to do his work, as they used to say, right. And that's why the bosses went after him. They attacked him because he wanted to do his work too well. He was unhealthy to have around. The speed-up might irk the other men but they would be unprepared, as most men are, from confusion and the hundred costs the family is heir to, to do anything. They would go along, even though it meant they'd wither and go dead. My father's threat to the bosses was not so much his activity as himself. he was an image to the other men of what they had been, a trace to the younger men of what work was. He had to be harassed.

Today he'd be fired. Or not hired in the first place. Or, if a company had to show a payroll for a contract, be the first laid off. Ground has been lost. But a good worker still knows, and can tell you, what my father knew. He just happened to be one of the first, and it was clearer earlier in the postal service than in heavy industry. He was at the switch point when the turn came. He was no enemy. He was opposition. He was fighting for pride in work which is personality. It is that simple. We have forgotten what men crave. We think that all workers want is pay. But that's all they are left with, where production, and that rot of modern work, efficiency, rule. Give workers only that and they'll featherbed you back. If you take away pride you'll have to give prizes. And why not? Corner men and they are good animals: they know how to resist.

Behind his bosses were the postal inspectors. Behind them Burleson. Behind Burleson the huge forfeit of pro-duction. It is old George Harris' proposition: bishops eats elders, elders eats common peopil, they eats sich cattil as me, I eats possums, possums eats chickins, chick-ins swallers wums, an' wums is content to eat dus, an' dus is the aind uv hit all.

Only hit ain't. The dus is the kulchur daid on the groun'. For example. My father was old fashion. He had notions having to do with courtesy, modesty, care, proportion, respect. He had them confused with his work. A letter, say. He was scrupulous about a letter. He had the idea it was somehow important just because it was made up of words (he had the notion that words have value, as signs of meaning and feeling) and because it was a communi-cation between two persons (the idea of a person seems to have meant something to him). Thus he took himself seriously as the last, and only directly personal agent, of several hired by a stamp to see that a letter reached the person to whom it was addressed or, rather (as I am sure he, with his notions, would have put it) for whom it was meant.

As a part of such motion he took himself to be respon-sible. (He was. I have known him, of an evening after work, to be as concerned as to whether a party on his route had got a letter they had been expecting which he had had to leave in their box because they were not at home, as another man might be concerned about well, say, the safe, or whether he had locked the office door.) A good carrier did not jam cards. He did not leave insured parcels carelessly. He stopped to ring and wait to get the mail inside when the weather was bad. He held mail for people when they were away, or forwarded for them, without delay. The niceties.

And the accommodations: bring stamps to people, or take their letters and buy the stamps for them. Or small packages or magazines, where they did not know the weight. Even a laundry, once in a while.

And registered mail: to let people know they could send money directly by you instead of going up town to the post office to do it, as most people think they have to. The finish on the work. (It was my father who first told me the answer of the cabinet maker to the looker-on who was making fun of the care the c.m. was giving to the under side of a table. "Why bother your self. No one will ever, in this world, notice that." Drawls the c.m., switching his chaw, "I notice it."

All of which courtesies take took time.

Enter: the route inspector.

From 1920 on my father was never left long at peace on his route without there was, suddenly, any day, a route inspector on his back. As he would leave the Post Office for his route there would be some guy, known or unknown, with his sheet of paper and his yellow look (the look of the checker in any business) who would go the route with him that day to "clock him," to count the pieces and the time. It was the way the bosses hounded a man, in Post Office talk.

They had another trick. When a man went on vacation they'd assign a special substitute to carry the route, a man whom the regulars called a route-killer, some bird who wanted to stand in with the foreman of carriers to get extra work and who was ready, for that reason, or from plain fear, to run around the route and get in under the regular's time. I had one once myself. He managed a ball club. A route was something he got rid of as soon as he could (though he was paid, as I was, by the hour) in order to have time to chew the fat with his players at noon or get the bases out to the field at night. He came in one day two hours under my time! That finished me on that route. They transferred me to a truck!

But I was a kid, and didn't care. With my father it was different. It was his life work. He got so he was grim and dangerous over this business. If he'd have been a machinist, they had turned him into such a bitter, revengeful man, he would have gone beyond the slow-down. He would have turned saboteur, and wrecked machinery. As it was he went illegal. He worked out a trick to beat them. It was to increase the mail the day they inspected him. He did it in one of two ways. On at least one occasion (at the height of his trouble, I'd say, from the way I remember it) when he was tipped off ahead of time that he was going to get it, he mailed first class stuff himself the night before, in several different handwritings to people on the route. Another time, it seems to me, he called my mother during the morning and had her drop some similar letters he had ready in order to fatten the afternoon delivery on his route. But the other device was simpler. It rested on the increase of advertising circulars in the 20s and 30s. It was mostly third class mail, and carriers were not obliged to deliver it the day it came in, if such a piece meant adding distance to the route. But my father went much further in his determination to beat the inspection system. He would cull out these circulars until he had a selected bunch of them well distributed around his route. These he would keep hidden in his locker or perhaps it was behind his sorting case at the post office. When an inspector was due out with him he would sort these pieces in with the day's mail. It took up the slack. (I should make clear that it was the custom, when the higher-ups were after a man, to send an inspector out at that time of the month or the week when the mail is lightest. Monday is such a day. The first of the month is the heaviest.)

It was a mischievous business, and my father lived with it nervously. (He had a bad time of it the day he discovered new cases had arrived and there had been some shifting of the old ones during the morning when he was out on the route.) My impression is, this stupid bundle of mail was on his mind all the years up to his death. There it sat, the only illegal thing he'd ever done, the one thing, and the only thing, if they found it, which would give them the goods they wished they had on him. His record was clean, clean as a whistle is the way he would have put it, if he was of a mind to talk about himself. Yet here he himself ran the risk of giving them the very thing they wanted. And why? Merely to beat them at a game which he took as an insult to his amour propre.

This is what I meant by his stubbornness. He wanted his route the way it had been before the speed-up. He wanted his route the way he had built it, with time left in for the courtesies, the niceties, and a coffee now and then. But there was a side to this desire, after his trouble, which has to be put this way: he wanted it the way it had been because the bosses wanted it different. The fact of the matter is he wanted to overprove his point with some idea that in so doing he made more apparent the dirtiness of their attack on him. Which, of course, was not so. He could easily have turned the point of any of their tricks by merely continuing as he had been. He had a long route and no one could have squeezed it much. The proof is, that when they finally decided he had suffered enough, after the Plymouth deal, they put him back on the route pretty much, as far as I can remember, as he had been beforehand. In other words the hounding took. The only thing it didn't do was break his will. He didn't give in. He only died.

It took fourteen years. The demerits came first. Then the removal from the route. At that point they pulled another military move. They required him to tear off the three red stars from his sleeve, for the fifteen years he had served. For they had a final ignominy. I suppose it is possible they thought they could drive him out of the service altogether. Anyhow they assigned him to the lowest job there is, the job the greenest sub carrier gets, the night collection.

I don't remember how long they kept him on it. It may have been a year. I'm not sure, now that I am further down into the past, if I am right they took him off his route immediately on our return from Plymouth. I'm not sure they didn't inspect the life out of him first, having docked his pay, and that it wasn't on one of these inspections that he called Paddy Hehir or maybe it was Blocky Sheehan a son of a bitch. In any case the night collection was the final punishment.

One thing stands out, a picture that Dinny Riordan gave me the day my father died. It was a sudden death, cerebral hemorrhage, the first shock on a Thursday paralyzing the right side, the second one, Saturday morning, getting the heart. What Dinny revealed to me was that in 1920, apparently not long after the start of the trouble, he and my father were on a streetcar going to their routes. (Dinny's was the next above the route adjoining my father's.) Suddenly as they were sitting there in the long seat at the back of the car Dinny became aware that my father was not listening to him, was in fact leaning slightly against him and looking off with a fixed look out the windows across the aisle. He thought my father was joking, or something, and gave him a shove. It was the way my father came out of it that made Dinny first aware that something was wrong. He said nothing, and nothing more was mentioned about it. But the doctors told me, when I checked with them, that it was the premonitory shock. The trouble had brought it on. Shortly after, in going over my father's papers, I discovered that it was the very year, 1920, that had begun the annual checkups with the doctor which were dramatized for me by the urine bottle.

The nights must have been dirt in my father's mouth, the city's main streets, letters in lumps, people to ask why he was there. Or to say, what's this we see in the papers. For he fought back from the start. The senator was David I. Walsh. He tried to reach him. The congressman was Pehr Holmes, a Swede. He saw him. Promises, letters, meetings, articles. The NALC. The branch of UNIPOX (Un. PO Clerks). I don't figure, now, that it was long before he was back on the route. But that, alas, was not the end of the struggle. It never ended for him. Somehow he had to pay them back, Hehir, Sheehan, and the Postmaster, Healy. He increased his work in the Branch. He widened out to the national officers. He joined the Carl the 15th Lodge, the Swedish American Federation. The paper *Svea* had helped in the struggle. He became a friend of Karl Fredin the editor. His Swedish began to come back. He began to get me to speak to their festivals. He became more and more involved. More evenings went out from his drawing, his piano playing. The one thing he did not lessen was Gloucester. Gloucester became the one offset. He would come each weekend, arranging rides for himself if he could, or hopping the train. Only in Gloucester was he free from revenge. And it was from Gloucester that he left the last time I saw him whole. He was to go the next weekend to the National Convention of the Carriers at Cleveland. It was to be a big business, for he and his cronies around the country (he had built up a terrific correspondence) were hoping they could turn out the old officers and put in Ferd Douglas of Brooklyn. It was one of the payoffs my father intended, for the officers of the NALC had failed him, he thought, in his fight. He was out to get them. It was to be a big thing, and when he was leaving he waked me to ask if I would let him take my suitcase which was bigger and newer than his. I had a use for it that coming weekend which seemed important to me, and I refused. He went away sore, and the curious thing is, that though my mother and I drove the hundred miles to the hospital the moment we heard he was sick and though I was with him much of the time until he died, I do not remember that he ever addressed me or seemed to notice that I was there. He pinched my mother's nose and said something unintelligible from the twist of his mouth but it is only now that I realize at no time did he admit a notice of me. Or do I exaggerate and punish myself anew for the guilt of my refusal of the suitcase. I do not know. What I do know is that the house, when we got back to it, showed that all that week he must have stayed up night after night preparing the papers and resolutions that were to be used at the Convention. That was 1934. Plymouth was all those years back, yet here he was locked in the struggle which issued from it. He had won the fight, and lost it, god help us all.

Grey Fox Books

John Coriolan	*Christy Dancing*
Margaret Cruikshank	*New Lesbian Writing*
Daniel Curzon	*Human Warmth & Other Stories*
Guy Davenport	*Herakleitos and Diogenes* *The Mimes of Herondas*
Edward Dorn	*Selected Poems*
Lawrence Ferlinghetti	*The Populist Manifesto*
Allen Ginsberg	*Composed on the Tongue* *The Gates of Wrath: Rhymed Poems 1948–1952* *Gay Sunshine Interview* (with Allen Young)
Howard Griffin	*Conversations with Auden*
Richard Hall	*Couplings: A Book of Stories* *Three Plays for a Gay Theater*
Jack Kerouac	*Heaven & Other Poems*
Stanley Lombardo	*Parmenides and Empedocles*
Michael McClure	*Hymns to St. Geryon & Dark Brown*
Frank O'Hara	*Early Writing* *Poems Retrieved* *Standing Still and Walking in New York*
Charles Olson	*The Post Office*
Eric Rofes	*"I Thought People Like That Killed Themselves"—Lesbians, Gay Men & Suicide*
Michael Rumaker	*A Day and a Night at the Baths* *My First Satyrnalia*
Gary Snyder	*He Who Hunted Birds in His Father's Village: Dimensions of a Haida Myth*
Gary Snyder, Lew Welch & Philip Whalen	*On Bread & Poetry*

Jack Spicer	*One Night Stand & Other Poems*
Samuel Steward	*Chapters from an Autobiography*
Lew Welch	*How I Work as a Poet & Other Essays* *I, Leo—An Unfinished Novel* *I Remain: The Letters of Lew Welch & the Correspondence of His Friends* *Ring of Bone: Collected Poems* *Selected Poems*
Philip Whalen	*Decompressions: Selected Poems* *Enough Said: Poems 1974–1979* *Scenes of Life at the Capital*
Allen Young	*Gays Under the Cuban Revolution*